Come Hear the Song of the Shepherd

An Interactive 30 Day Journey Through Psalm 23

by Jamie De Silvia

Bri -
may this book
draw you ever
closer to Jesus.
♡ Jamie
De Silvia

Table of Contents

Before You Begin

This devotional book was born out of an in-depth bible study on Psalm 23 (the famous *The Lord is my Shepherd* psalm) that I taught last year. There are so many good nuggets of truth in this familiar passage that are life-changing! I pray that you are blessed and transformed by the Song of the Shepherd.

I share many of my own experiences in the text so that you can see how the principles of Psalm 23 have played out in my life. I'm no expert, and certainly not perfect. I am a work in progress. I want to be real with you in hopes that you can relate to the principles being taught throughout the text.

There is no magic in this book—only the opportunity to grow closer and to go deeper with God. It is possible to connect with God and receive personal guidance and encouragement from Him. I write much in this book about hearing from God, allowing Him to guide me in making decisions, and learning specific things from Him. If this is a foreign concept to you, I'd like to try to explain!

I'm going to give an example of what it can be like to hear from God. The comparison isn't perfect, so bear with me, but I think it may help if you are unfamiliar with recognizing the whisper of God in your life.

Hearing from God is similar to the experience of "hearing" a loved one's voice who is not with you at the moment. You may see something that reminds you of them, and it can feel like some sort of sign. You might be reminded of something they said or did in the past, and in that moment, you feel close to them even though they might be miles away or gone to heaven. Perhaps you are not even thinking about them, but something they regularly say will just pop in your head. (This is something I pray that my children will experience regularly! What would Mom say right now?!?) You hear the person's voice in your mind— it's not audible, but you hear it. It may feel like they've sent you some encouragement or guidance. All of this happens in your mind, in a matter of moments, but it's real.

Because God's Spirit lives within the person who believes that Jesus is his or her Savior, this Holy Spirit can remind a person of things that God or Jesus said in the Bible, or things He has already promised or communicated in the past. His voice can come like a thought popping in one's head, a memory resurfacing, or similar to what one might call intuition. It is usually very quiet and gentle but can also be very persistent. To me, this experience is far more powerful than the example I gave about a loved one, but it is a close example of how I have personally heard His voice.

When you read this book, especially the quotations from the Bible, you may sense a quickening or stirring in you that bears witness to the truth of what you are reading. Let that stirring have a voice— it may be God speaking to you. It may seem strange, or you may think it's all hype or nonsense, but I challenge you to allow God to speak to you in your heart, and I hope that you will respond to Him. If you want to know more about having a relationship with God, turn to the last section of this book.

You will see this symbol ❀ throughout the book. It indicates a question or an activity for you to expand your understanding of the verses or experience God's presence in a tangible way. Please give the activities a try, even if you think they are unusual! Feel free to write in the spaces provided.

This book is designed for you to read on your own, allowing time to develop your spiritual life. The book would also be great for a group! Read on your own and then buddy up with a friend or two to discuss what you are learning and experiencing in your individual time with God. Are you in a Bible study group? Plan to discuss a few days' worth of completed readings at your meeting. The questions will create plenty of discussion during your meeting time together.

Day 1: The Song of the Shepherd

Psalm 23 is one of the most commonly quoted Bible passages of all time. It is heard at funerals, quoted in movies, featured in greeting cards and on gift items. Perhaps because it is so common and familiar, most of us rush by it in our reading of the Bible. We know what it says and what it means, so we hurry on to other passages that we hope contain some new insight.

Perhaps shepherding is too far removed from our modern daily experiences. Psalm 23 may be a passage that we don't readily connect with since we do not know the intricacies of the shepherd life, especially that of ancient times. So, we rush on to other passages that seem more relevant.

When God first asked me to teach an in-depth study on Psalm 23 that would result in five or six weekly lessons, I was doubtful. I didn't think there was enough material in Psalm 23 for a study that long. I was so wrong! How often we are limited by our own perspectives and preferences.

My initial thoughts stemmed from the misleading familiarity that I had with the psalm, as well as my propensity to rush by the passage in search of something new. God challenged me to look for something new right there in the familiar. He also brought to my attention the fact that we "hear" the psalm in David's voice, but in reality, all of Scripture is inspired by God. What if we read the passage anew, and thought of it as God speaking?

꙾ Permit me to change the wording in Psalm 23. Slow down, allow your heart and mind to be open, and hear *His* voice singing the Song of the Shepherd. Take your time, reading more than one time.

I am the Lord your Shepherd.

In My care, you shall not want for anything.

I am inviting you lie down in My lush green pastures.

I am leading you beside quiet, calming waters.

I am refreshing and restoring your soul.

I am guiding you along righteous paths for the sake of My name.

Even though you may walk through the darkest valleys, you will fear no evil.

Why? Because I AM with you.

My shepherd's rod and staff bring comfort to you.

I am preparing a bountiful table before you in the presence of your enemies.

I am anointing your head with oil.

Your cup is overflowing.

Surely My goodness and love follow you all the days of your life.

You will dwell in My house, with Me, forever.

🌀 What is the Shepherd saying to you right now?   What is He inviting you to do?

Day 2: The Shepherd's Sufficiency

God uses many metaphors throughout the Bible to describe Himself and His relationship with us. In the pages of Scripture, He describes Himself as a Teacher, Master, Lord, Farmer, Gardener, King, Lover, Savior, Husband, Father, Judge, and more. He uses these word pictures to give us a clearer understanding of His character and His role in our lives.

In Psalm 23, we see God describing Himself as a Shepherd. He reveals details about Himself in this psalm. If we linger long enough in the verses, we will see His Shepherd heart and the compassion He has for His sheep. The purpose of this book is to create an opportunity for you to know Him in a deeper way. I believe that He will reveal very specific and personal insight to you as we delve in together.

I'd like to take a few moments to share what the resounding theme of Psalm 23 has been for me personally. Since my teenage years, I have spent the bulk of my energy trying to control my life and perform everything in it perfectly. Unfortunately, for a long time, this kept me from truly trusting in the Lord and fulling leaning on Him.

Years ago, when God was developing and expanding the gift of teaching in me, my perfectionist ways and desire for control started to get in the way. I'll never forget the morning that I was praying on the treadmill, and God spoke to me so firmly and clearly:

If you do not lay down your self-sufficiency, there is not much more that I can do with you. I've taken you as far as I can, unless you are willing to release control and find your suffi- ciency in ME alone.

I'd like to say that I responded with a passionate "Yes, Lord! I will lay it all down for you!" but I did not. I came completely unraveled at the thought of laying down control of my life. I was independent and stubborn, fearful of relying on anyone but myself. Control was the only thing that helped me manage the brokenness in my life. It was the only thing that I thought would keep the fear and pain at bay.

But another fear came—fear that I would not be able to serve God the way that I longed to. I eventually began to yield to God and asked Him to show me what a life of dependency, rather than self-sufficiency, looked like. One day at a time, I worked on putting my full trust in Him instead of seeking control. Psalm 23 came along during that journey and I began to see the sheep and shepherd as a clear picture of what dependency, and a life of God-sufficiency, looks like.

❧ One of the most telling things I learned from Psalm 23 came from looking at the verbs in the passage. Take a look for yourself. Underline any verbs/actions you see in the following passage.

The Lord is my shepherd, I shall not want. He makes me lie down in green pastures, He leads me beside quiet waters, He restores my soul. He guides me in paths of righteousness for His name's sake. Even though I walk through the valley of the shadow of death, I fear no evil, for You are with me. Your rod and Your staff, they comfort me. You prepare a table before me in the presence of my enemies. You have anointed my head with oil; my cup overflows. Surely goodness and loving-kindness (mercy) will follow me all the days of my life, and I will dwell in the house of the Lord forever.   *Psalm 23, NASB*

✾ Who seems to be doing most of the action?

✾ What does that mean for you?

I'm sure you noticed that God is doing most of the action! As His sheep, we are in a position of trusting and receiving more than anything else. God used this Song of the Shepherd to show me what a life of complete trust and dependency looks like.

God wants us to take all the energy we spend on worrying, controlling circumstances and people, positioning ourselves, or performing for worthiness, and instead, focus that energy into trusting Him, yielding to Him, hoping in Him, and resting in Him. We must stop thinking ourselves so responsible for everything. We will see that sheep are responsible for very little!

✾ What will God show you as we hover over the verses of Psalm 23 and listen for His voice? Begin to pray that He will open your eyes and ears to receive His communication. Pray that your heart will be open to new insights and challenges that He will present to you. Pray for the willingness to walk in the truth that He will reveal as you listen to the Song of the Shepherd.

12

Day 3: Praying the Song of the Shepherd

Perhaps you are starting to be aware of areas of your life where you tend to rely on your own strength or perspective. The Lord may be calling you to trust Him a bit more and lay down control. All that is required from us on this journey from self-sufficiency to more dependency on God is a willingness to grow. Even if you are frightened at the thought of letting go, or feel like you have no idea how to stop doing things the way you always have, just ask Him to show you what to do. He will lead you one step at a time.

When I first became aware of my need to stop living in self-sufficiency, I had no idea how to change my ways. As I was confronted with fear and the urge to seize control of people and situations in my daily life, I was prompted by the Holy Spirit to pray aloud, "I put my trust in You, Lord." I'd pray it again and again as a push back against my desires to fix, change, or control the things in my life that felt out of control. On especially difficult days, I took to praying only one word: JESUS. I would call his name to remind myself that He is in control and that He will always do what is best for me.

🌀 Take a few minutes and pray through Psalm 23. If you've never prayed through Scripture before, don't worry. It's very simple! Just read each verse and then rephrase it into a prayer. For example, verse 1 could be rephrased as, "*Lord, thank you for being my Shepherd. I want to put my full trust in You to provide for all my needs.*" On the next page, you'll find one of my favorite translations of Psalm 23. You can use that for your prayer, or turn to your own Bible to do so.

The Lord is my Shepherd [to feed, guide, and shield me], I shall not lack.

He makes me lie down in [fresh, tender] green pastures;

He leads me beside the still and restful waters.

He refreshes and restores my life;

He leads me in the paths of righteousness [uprightness and right standing with Him— not for my earning it, but] for His name's sake.

Yes, though I walk through the [deep, sunless] valley of the shadow of death, I will fear or dread no evil, for You are with me;

Your rod [to protect] and Your staff [to guide], they comfort me.

You prepare a table before me in the presence of my enemies.

You anoint my head with oil; my [brimming] cup runs over.

Surely or only goodness, mercy, and unfailing love shall follow me all the days of my life,

and through the length of my days the house of the Lord [and His presence] shall be my dwelling place.

Psalm 23, Amplified Bible, Classic Edition

🌀 What part of this prayer do you feel the need to repeat on a regular basis?

Day 4: The Work of the Shepherd

Historically, shepherding has been a lowly occupation. In large families with land and livestock, shepherding duties were passed from one son to the next as the older sons married or took on other, more important roles in the family. Shepherd duties eventually fell to the youngest son.[1] Moving sheep to seasonal pastures required the shepherding son to be out with the flocks for long periods of time. It is fair to say that this occupation was a lonely one. Perhaps it was the fields far from home where David's heart for God developed—in seasons of time alone with the Lord and his sheep.

The livelihood of the shepherd rested in his flocks. Sheep were acquired by purchasing or by breeding, which made each sheep valuable to him. A good shepherd became very familiar with the ways of sheep. He had to understand the biology, behavior patterns, and needs of the flock. Due to their familiarity, shepherds were not surprised or shocked by the behavior of the sheep. In fact, they learned to anticipate what the animals would do in any scenario.

Likely the most important component of shepherding was **proximity** (nearness). Tending sheep was a hands-on occupation that required a strong presence and a close eye on the flock to monitor feeding and safety. Shepherds did not leave their sheep unattended. This quality—proximity to the sheep—is what makes our Lord the perfect Shepherd. God is always near, always close. He has promised us that He will never leave us or forsake us.

Know that the Lord is God. It is he who made us, and we are his; we are his people, the sheep of his pasture. Psalm 100:3

He tends his flock like a shepherd: He gathers the lambs in his arms and carries them close to his heart; he gently leads those that have young. Isaiah 40:11

So why are there times when we feel far from Him? If He is truly always near, then the distance we feel must be perceived only, and not real. Perhaps we let our feelings influence our perception here. All we need to do when we are feeling far from the Shepherd is to recognize how close He already is. When we acknowledge His current proximity, our feelings or perception of distance will dissipate.

๑ Are you feeling far from God? Recognize the Shepherd's close presence right now and talk to Him.

๑ How has God's love and care for you been like a shepherd caring for His sheep?

๑ How do you feel about being one of His sheep?

Day 5: The Shepherd's Flock

Let's talk about sheep. The domesticated varieties are not self-sufficient creatures. They are quite dependent on their shepherd for feeding, watering, wound care, and protection from predators. Sheep are prone to wander and scatter. They tend to be fretful and fearful animals, either becoming paralyzed with fear or running when danger presents itself.[2] Sheep often get themselves in places they can't get out of, needing the shepherd to rescue them. They aren't capable of tending their own wounds. What a perfect picture of dependency they are.

> ...By his wounds you have been healed. For you were like sheep going astray, but now you have returned to the Shepherd and Overseer of your souls. I Peter 3:24c-25

Living in this world, we know deep down that we are as defenseless as sheep. As if our own sin and failure did not create enough need for a Shepherd, we face predators and enemies in this life that can hurt us. We get lost just like sheep do, needing to be rescued out of predicaments and pits along the way. We need to be guided and cared for. When we can truly see ourselves as sheep, there is comfort and freedom in recognizing our great need for the Shepherd and giving up the instinct to self-guide, self-protect, and self-sustain.

⑨ Read through Psalm 23 on the next page and jot down any duties or responsibilities that you see for both the shepherd and the sheep.

> The Lord is my shepherd, I shall not want. He makes me lie down in green pastures, He leads me beside quiet waters, He

restores my soul. He guides me in paths of righteousness for His name's sake. Even though I walk through the valley of the shadow of death, I fear no evil, for You are with me. Your rod and Your staff, they comfort me. You prepare a table before me in the presence of my enemies. You have anointed my head with oil; my cup overflows. Surely goodness and loving-kindness (mercy) will follow me all the days of my life, and I will dwell in the house of the Lord forever.   Psalm 23, NASB

Duties/Responsibilities

<u>Shepherd</u>   <u>Sheep</u>

✤ What are your thoughts about the balance of duties?

✤ Talk to the Shepherd with that in mind.

Day 6: Jehovah Shepherds

A Psalm of David. The Lord is my shepherd, I shall not want.
{Psalm 23:1}

Verse one begins with very simple language. First, we see the author's declaration: this is a Psalm of David. The next few words have little else but subject and verb. It literally reads in the Hebrew as *Jehovah shepherds*. What a bold and profound truth. He is the Shepherd, and shepherding is what He does. Jehovah shepherds you.

Psalm 23 is not the only Bible passage to describe God as a Shepherd. Let's look at Ezekiel 34 and see what makes Him the ideal Shepherd.

...The Sovereign Lord says: Woe to you shepherds of Israel who only take care of yourselves! Should not shepherds take care of the flock? You eat the curds, clothe yourselves with the wool and slaughter the choice animals, but you do not take care of the flock. You have not strengthened the weak or healed the sick or bound up the injured. You have not brought back the strays or searched for the lost. You have ruled them harshly and brutally. So they were scattered because there was no shepherd, and when they were scattered, they became food for all the wild animals. My sheep wandered over all the mountains and on every high hill. They were scattered over the whole earth, and no one searched or looked for them.

For this is what the Sovereign Lord says: I myself will search for my sheep and look after them. As a shepherd looks after his scattered flock when he is with them, so will I look after my sheep. I will rescue them from all the places where they were scattered on a day of clouds and darkness. I will bring them out from the nations and gather them from the countries, and I will bring them into their own land. I will pasture them on the mountains of Israel, in the ravines and in all the settlements in the land. I will tend them in good pasture, and the mountain heights of Israel will be their grazing land. There they will lie down in good grazing land, and there they will feed in a rich pasture on the mountains of Israel. I myself will tend my sheep and have them lie down, declares the Sovereign Lord. I will search for the lost and bring back the strays. I will bind up the injured and strengthen the weak... Ezekiel 34:1-6, 11-16a

✿ What qualities do you see that make the Lord a Good Shepherd?

The first part this Ezekiel passage is a word of criticism to the human shepherds who were appointed to lead God's people. This is some harsh language that reveals God's heart for His people, His sheep. It is clear what God thinks a shepherd should do, and He prides Himself on doing these things for His people. He strengthens the weak, heals the sick, and binds up the injured. He brings back the strays and searches for the lost. He does not rule them harshly and brutally. He does not want them to be scattered or to wander.

The verses that follow the criticism in Ezekiel 34 show God's desire to care for us, to meet our needs, to lead us, to tend to us individually and lovingly. We see His intent to heal and bless us in the high places of life (mountains) as well as the low places (ravines).

This passage also reveals God's understanding of the nature of sheep. He recognizes that they are easily scattered, that they are often lost and wounded. He is not surprised by their nature. In fact, when looking at the passage more closely, we see that the word of correction is reserved for the shepherds only. He doesn't criticize the sheep for getting lost or being weak and wounded. He understands their ways. This understanding gives way to compassion and mercy.

God takes great care in knowing our ways. As a recovering perfectionist, I tend to be hyper aware of my weaknesses. I have always gone through seasons of drifting or running from the Lord, and I have been very critical of myself regarding that. For a long time, I was trapped in a cycle of perfectionism: I would press into the Lord with faith and gusto, then fail to meet my unrealistic expectations, shame myself, wander aimlessly, and then finally drag myself back to Him and start all over again. God began to show me this pattern in Scripture (Hello, book of Judges!) and He let me know that everyone experiences some form of this cycle of seeking Him, eventually drifting, wandering or running, then recognizing the need for Him and returning to intimacy with Him. God made it clear that I need to understand my pattern (like He does) rather than shame myself for it. By recognizing my pattern, I learned to give myself the grace that He gives. When grace won out over shame, the cycle began to settle down. I began to drift away less, for shorter distances, come back sooner, and be more aware of what caused me to run or drift in the first place.

Ezekiel 34 confirms that God knows your pattern. He sees it; He is willing to pursue you and restore you. He is willing to be patient when you are running or hiding. He knows that you are like a sheep that runs in fear and gets lost in the process. He loves you and understands your ways.

🌀 What kind of spiritual patterns or cycles do you experience?

✺ Review the second half of the verses from Ezekiel 34 and write down the phrases that speak to you. Try writing them in personal form, as though God were speaking them to you. For example: "*I will rescue you from all the places you have been scattered to.*" Allow the Lord to speak to you in a specific way as you write the phrases out.

Day 7: Jesus, the Good Shepherd

The Lord is my shepherd, I shall not want. {Psalm 23:1}

In John 10, Jesus describes Himself as the *Good Shepherd*.

The one who enters by the gate is the shepherd of the sheep. The gatekeeper opens the gate for him, and the sheep listen to his voice. He calls his own sheep by name and leads them out. When he has brought out all his own, he goes on ahead of them, and his sheep follow him because they know his voice.

I am the good shepherd. The good shepherd lays down his life for the sheep. The hired hand is not the shepherd and does not own the sheep. So when he sees the wolf coming, he abandons the sheep and runs away. Then the wolf attacks the flock and scatters it. The man runs away because he is a hired hand and cares nothing for the sheep. I am the good shepherd; I know my sheep and my sheep know me—just as the Father knows me and I know the Father—and I lay down my life for the sheep. John 10:2-4, 11-15

  ❀   What qualities do you notice that make Jesus a Good Shepherd?

Jesus reiterates some of the same themes that we saw yesterday in Ezekiel 34. He makes a comparison between Himself and others that don't measure up to His care. It is very clear that He loves the sheep, that He knows them intimately, and would do anything for them. Perhaps Jesus is such a Good Shepherd because He knows what it's like to be a sheep—to be human. As a man, he battled temptation and understands the weaknesses of the human mind and heart. Because of that, we should never hesitate to come to the Shepherd and approach Him, to sit in His pasture, to open our hearts to Him.

🌀 What do you love most about your Shepherd?

🌀 Are you aware that He understands your weaknesses and the things you are going through? Ask him for confirmation of that if you need to.

🌀 Jesus calls His sheep by name. Can you hear Him calling you by name? Is He calling you by any other special name(s)? Close your eyes and listen for a moment.

Day 8: Waiting is Not Lacking

The Lord is my shepherd, I shall not want. {Psalm 23:1}

After he declares that God is his Shepherd, David recognizes that this results in his needs being fully met. Different translations of this part of verse 1 read as *I shall not want, I lack nothing, He gives me everything I need*, or *I always have more than enough.* These statements are loaded with faith and contentment! The Hebrew phrase used in this verse is also used in Deuteronomy when God promises that there will be no lack in the promised land.

Observe the commands of the Lord your God, walking in obedience to him and revering him.

*For the Lord your God is bringing you into a good land—a land with brooks, streams, and deep springs gushing out into the valleys and hills, a land with wheat and barley, vines and fig trees, pomegranates, olive oil and honey; a land where bread will not be scarce and **you will lack nothing**; a land where the rocks are iron and you can dig copper out of the hills.*

When you have eaten and are satisfied, praise the Lord your God for the good land he has given you. Deuteronomy. 8:6-10

What a beautiful glimpse of all that God wants to generously provide for His people! Not only in the Promised Land of Israel centuries ago, and not only in His pasture, but in the everyday lives of His people today.

As we wrestle to understand this idea of lacking nothing, we must put "lack" into perspective. When my oldest daughter came home from a mission trip to Kenya, Africa, she was astounded by the joy she saw in children who appeared to lack everything! Here in

America, in the land of plenty, we have more than we need—more than we know what to do with. Yet, if I were to ask you to tell me something that you felt you were lacking, I bet you would be able to come up with at least one thing. I'm sure that I would! It might not be material; it could be emotional or relational or spiritual. Sadly, while we live in the land of plenty, we are often plagued by what we don't have or what is out of reach.

Friend, if you do not have a certain thing right now, it is either because it is not something that God thinks is best for you (and He is going to give you something else) or it is not the right time for you to have it. We spend a good part of our lives in a waiting pattern: waiting for answers to our questions or problems, waiting for provision for our needs, waiting for a breakthrough in an area of struggle, waiting for doors to open or close, waiting for healing, or waiting for resolution. I would venture to say that I have done more waiting in this life than anything else. Waiting can be long and hard. But hear me now: *waiting is not lacking.* Waiting means that the thing is coming because your Shepherd plans to provide. God rarely schedules provision ahead of time; He likes for His delivery to coincide with the greatest hour of need.

Waiting is crucial for the development of our character. Imagine if we never had to wait our turn as children. What a world of spoiled creatures we would be! Waiting is the arena in which we train to set aside our own plans and control. Waiting is the soil where our trust in God grows, thrives, and multiplies. Our needs and wants provide everyday opportunities to develop dependence on God.

So, what are you waiting for? Are you waiting for that thing with worry and anxiety, or are you waiting with expectancy and hope? Continue to present your need or lack to Him in prayer and begin to thank Him in advance for the way He will answer. It may not come the way you've imagined it! God has a way of doing things in unexpected and extraordinary ways.

In the late 2000's our family suffered serious financial hardship along with many other Americans. For months, we were unable to make our house payment, but since the mortgage company was backlogged with foreclosures, we were able to stay a long time in our home without making a payment. After a couple of unsuccessful attempts to refinance and catch up, we prepared to lose our home completely. At the time, I was a few months away from delivering our son and we didn't know where we would go.

During that time, my husband had lunch with a friend who said that he felt compelled by the Lord to help us. He offered to buy our house from the bank and then he and his wife wanted to rent it to us until we got back on our feet. The goal was for us to buy the house back from them when we were ready.

We were so shocked! After 18 months of hardship, we had let the house go from our hearts and were looking for any simple provision the Lord would offer in our time of great need. We had NO expectation to be able to stay in our house! The sale went through and closed just a few weeks before our son was born. We were blown away to have such a lavish provision, so blessed to have friends walk alongside us and be a part of the provision. Several years later, we did buy the house back. The whole experience truly felt like a miracle!

God has a way of weaving our lives together so that we get to wait together, celebrate together, and even be the vessel of provision for each other. Waiting on God in dependency can be a glorious thing—even though the world thinks that being dependent on others is a negative thing. The Shepherd longs for your dependency on Him, and He will use your needs to teach you how to lay down self-sufficiency and learn to trust Him fully.

🌀 What are you waiting for right now?

🌀 Talk to your Shepherd about how you are feeling about the wait. Ask Him to help you trust, believe, and hope in Him.

Day 9: The Shepherd's Pasture

He makes me lie down in green pastures; He leads me beside quiet waters. {Psalm 23:2}

David's experience as a shepherd makes the writing of this psalm so beautiful—and accurate! The shepherd knows what sheep need and how to provide it for them. God clearly showed David some amazing spiritual parallels during the time he spent out in the fields as a young man making his sheep *lie down in green pastures* and leading them *beside quiet waters* (Psalm 23:2).

🌀 What comes to mind when you think of green pastures? Literally? Figuratively? Jot down your thoughts.

A couple of years ago, I took an oil painting class and discovered more God-given talent in myself than expected! My absolute favorite thing to paint is landscapes and trees because I love being outside in the beauty of creation. For me, the green pastures in Psalm 23:2 make me think of getting out in nature, away from the pressures and schedules of life, where I can rest my heart and mind. He speaks to me so distinctly through the elements of His creation: clouds, trees, birds, water. I think green pastures represent a time and place where I can breathe deeply and hear Him clearly.

Remember when we read about God's desire for His flock in Ezekiel 34? Let's review some of the verses to observe what He says about the pasture.

The Sovereign Lord says: I myself will search for my sheep and look after them. As a shepherd looks after his scattered flock when he is with them, so will I look after my sheep. I will rescue them from all the places where they were scattered on a day of clouds and darkness. I will bring them out from the nations and gather them from the countries, and I will bring them into their own land. I will pasture them on the mountains of Israel, in the ravines and in all the settlements in the land. I will tend them in a good pasture, and the mountain heights of Israel will be their grazing land. There they will lie down in good grazing land, and there they will feed in a rich pasture on the mountains of Israel. I myself will tend my sheep and have them lie down, declares the Sovereign Lord. Ezekiel 34:11-15

🌀 What do you notice about God's pasture?

What I find striking here is that the alternative to being in God's pasture is being lost, alone, and scattered in foreign places. When God gathers us into His pasture, we have a safe place to dwell, a place to belong, a place where we are cared for and protected within. We are home, no longer wandering or searching for safety. This is God's desire for us: to lay down and rest in His care.

Also notice that the pasture God speaks of is not just wide-open grassy spaces. There are high places in His pasture (the mountain heights) and there are low places in His pasture (the ravines). This passage calls us to let go of what we think the pasture should look like. It's clear that we can rest in Him whether we are experiencing the high points of victory or breakthrough, or the low points of suffering and loss. We can rest in His care at all points in between. It is not the terrain or the surroundings, **but the Shepherd's**

presence that makes a pasture home. It's His presence that makes it possible for us to rest, to be nourished, to be cared for.

In Psalm 23:2, David declares that God his Shepherd *makes me lie down in green pastures*. What irony in this statement! No person or animal can be made to lie down and rest if they do not want to do it. The only way to make someone rest is to coax them into it. Create an environment where they can settle down and recognize their own fatigue. I believe this is God's approach to our rest. He prepares the rest, invites us to it, but we must want it to enter His rest. There are times in our lives when we have not heeded His invitation to rest and He must then orchestrate circumstances to *make* us rest. That might include allowing illness, tragedy, injury, loss, closed doors, career changes, and the like to enter our lives and slow us down. God is imploring us today to enter His pasture and rest before He must make us do it. Make no mistake—this is not a threat. It is a loving invitation. Come and rest.

🌀 What is keeping you from laying down in His pasture and resting in His presence?

🌀 Be silent for a moment and tune into His invitation to rest. Jot down anything that you may sense or hear from the Lord.

Day 10: Quiet Waters

He makes me lie down in green pastures; He leads me beside quiet waters. {Psalm 23:2}

❀ What comes to mind when you think of quiet waters?

I recently went through a very difficult season with a family member and there were countless days when I felt wounded, angry, and grieved. At the time, I was walking several times a week to a nearby riverwalk. There, I would sit on a rock at the edge of the water, feeling miles away from all the things that troubled me. The water had such a calming effect; I was able to pray more clearly and hear the Lord's encouragement and guidance. I began the habit of selecting a nearby leaf or two that would represent a person or a situation that I needed to surrender control of. As I tossed them into the water and watched the leaves float downstream, I felt confident that the Lord was going to take care of those things that I had no control over. That physical act of dropping the leaf in the water, coupled with the soothing sounds of the stream, created such a healing process for me! God led me to the quiet waters of that little man-made stream just a mile from my suburban neighborhood and I will never forget what He did for me there, during such a difficult time.

🌀 Have you experienced a touch from God in a water environment? Perhaps on a boat, at the beach, near a waterfall or stream, or during a rainstorm? How did that impact you?

While water has the power to soothe, it also holds much symbolism in the Bible. It represents eternal life, cleansing, the Holy Spirit, and more. The absolute truth is that we cannot live without water! We need to drink water daily to keep our bodies operating, and we need the Living Water that God provides to thrive spiritually every day.

Sheep are dependent on their shepherd to lead them to water. Sheep cannot always discern healthy water from unhealthy water, so this part of the shepherd's care is crucial. Not only do they need safe water to drink, but sheep also need quiet waters, or slow streams to drink from. Rough waters pose a threat to sheep that may tumble in while trying to drink. Our Shepherd knows exactly what we need and provides living water for each of us. Even when we are not near water, the presence of His Holy Spirit can be like quiet waters in our hearts and minds.

🌀 Are you in need of calming, quiet waters today? Talk to the Lord about your need and ask Him to fulfill it. Be open to His leading.

Day 11: The Trouble with Rest

He makes me lie down in green pastures; He leads me beside quiet waters. {Psalm 23:2}

Psalm 23's imagery of green pastures and quiet streams accurately communicate our great need for REST. We are going to spend a couple of days talking about this important subject.

🌀 How do you define rest?

🌀 One definition of rest is *to cease work or movement in order to relax, refresh oneself, or recover strength.*[3] How are you doing when it comes to rest?

We often forget that we've been commanded to slow down on a regular basis:

There are six days when you may work, but the seventh day is a day of sabbath rest, a day of sacred assembly. You are not to do any work; wherever you live, it is a sabbath to the Lord. Leviticus 23:3

While this is written as a command, it's more importantly an invitation that God has extended to us. He knows how much we need to slow down and recuperate from our work—physically, mentally, emotionally, and spiritually. He wants to lighten our load

35

and revitalize us.

God instituted the sabbath on a weekly basis so that His people would get in the habit of resting regularly. He wanted us to find a rhythm of working six days, and then observing a day of worship and rest. When we do this, we begin to recognize what we can accomplish in a week and learn to take on only what we can finish in the time that we have. Regular observance of the sabbath rest leads to healthy habits and boundaries if we let the Lord teach us and lead us.

As humans, we put a high priority on our work and our responsibilities. When we are treading water in the sea of our lives, we rarely think that **rest** is the solution. We think that doing, fixing, planning, and finishing are the solutions. It may feel like we will lose control if we stop to rest. That is precisely the situation God's people found themselves in Isaiah 30. Both the kingdoms of Israel and Judah were being threatened by the neighboring nation of Assyria, but instead of seeking God and resting in Him, they were going to Egypt to make an alliance and gain support.

> *This is what the Sovereign Lord, the Holy One of Israel, says: "In repentance and rest is your salvation, in quietness and trust is your strength, but you would have none of it. You said, 'No, we will flee on horses (to Egypt).' Therefore, you will flee! You said, 'We will ride off on swift horses.'   Isaiah 30:15-16*

Like God's people, if we aren't resting it's likely because we are running. We are racing through schedules, running through plans and scenarios, and wearing ourselves out on the hamster wheel of worry. We are running—when rest, quietness, and trust in the Lord is the answer.

Rest requires releasing unfinished work, unresolved issues, and unanswered questions into God's hands. We have such a hard time letting go because we think that with the right approach and a little more time, we can fix it, resolve it, or tie up the loose ends. The

36

truth is that there will always be something hanging in the balance, so we must embrace the reality of unfinished business in order to be able to rest on a regular basis. Our ability to rest is directly related to our willingness to trust God with the things that are hard to lay down.

Rest isn't simply about laying **ourselves** down for a time. It's about laying down control, unresolved conflict, expectations, the need to know the future, the desire to change minds and circumstances, injustice, and more. God is inviting us to lay these things down in His capable hands and rest in His green pastures or beside His quiet waters.

🌀 What do you need to lay down in order to rest in the Lord today?

🌀 Talk to God about each of these things and lay them in His capable hands one at a time. Tune into what He says to you when you surrender them. Jot down anything you want to remember from this moment of trust and surrender.

Day 12: The Shepherd's Presence

*He makes me lie down in green pastures; He leads me beside
quiet waters. {Psalm 23:2}*

We've established that God's seemingly simple command to rest
is not always easy to do. As I studied references to rest throughout
Scripture, an insightful connection emerged.

My Presence will go with you and I will give you rest.
Exodus 33:14

This verse came out of the conversation that Moses had with God
as they prepared to embark on the journey to the promised land.
Moses was concerned that God would send them in, but not go with
them.   God's promise to go with them is very personal here. The
word He uses for presence is a Hebrew word that literally means
face. He is promising to personally walk with them and dwell close
to them. The result of being near His face or His presence is *rest*.
The people will have no worries about hunger or threats when the
Lord is going with them and dwelling with them.

*Whoever dwells in the shelter of the Most High will rest in the
shadow of the Almighty. I will say of the Lord, "He is my refuge
and my fortress, my God, in whom I trust." He will cover you
with his feathers, and under his wings you will find refuge; his
faithfulness will be your shield and rampart. Ps.91:1-2, 4*

Here we have a promise of rest for those who dwell close to God,
in His presence. The word for *shelter* is more often translated as
secret place. To find a secret place, one must search it and seek it
out. God wants us to seek His presence and then choose to stay
there as much as we can. The benefit of doing so is being able to

39

rest in His shadow, to rest under His wings. What a beautiful image! We can rest like a baby bird nestled under the wings of its parent.

When a shepherd offers rest to his sheep, the most important factor that will allow the flock to lay down in green pastures is his presence. He must be close by to assure them that they are safe enough to rest. They are truly dependent on the shepherd for this. We too are dependent on our Shepherd for rest. We must know and remember that He is close by. Our feelings may convince us otherwise, but His proximity is a fact.

꩜ There is no denying the connection between God's presence and the gift of rest. Think of a time when you felt the Lord's presence in a strong way. Did you feel at rest emotionally, physically or mentally?

꩜ Are you aware of His presence right now at this moment?

꩜ If you are not sure, I encourage you to try a simple activity with 3 steps. First, close your eyes and imagine that you are in one of your favorite places, where you feel at peace. Try to visualize all the details around you. Second, imagine Jesus walking up to you in that place. Third, allow Him to do or speak whatever is on His heart. Let the Holy Spirit guide you during this exercise.

꩜ Write down anything that you want to remember from this moment in His presence.

Day 13: The Shepherd's Yoke

He makes me lie down in green pastures; He leads me beside quiet waters. {Psalm 23:2}

Listen to what Jesus had to say about finding rest for our souls:

Come to me, all you who are weary and burdened, and I will give you rest. Take my yoke upon you and learn from me, for I am gentle and humble in heart, and you will find rest for your souls. For my yoke is easy and my burden is light.   Matthew 11:28-30

Read those words of Jesus and His invitation to rest one more time. Notice that we are to do three things: *Come. Take His yoke. Learn from Him.* In return, we will receive the rest that we so desperately need.

The first thing Jesus asks is to **come**. This might sound simple; don't we all come to Jesus at some point? Yet we often come as a last resort, when we have tried all that we know to do, but have failed. It took many years of walking with the Lord for me to realize that the invitation to come was for every day—all day! The problem is that self-sufficiency tells me to do everything in my own power to control and perform throughout my daily life. However, complete trust in Jesus requires that I come to Him every day, every hour.

Next, Jesus asks us to **take His yoke**. Perhaps you aren't familiar with a yoke. It's a device used since early Biblical times to connect a pair of animals together for the purpose of harnessing the strength of the two beasts at once. Typically, a yoke was used on oxen for pulling heavy objects and farming. What is lesser known about the yoke, is that it was also used to teach an inexperienced animal how to work. The younger animal was yoked with a stronger, more experienced beast and the stronger one would do most of the work while the student plodded along, learning both the rhythm of labor and the meaning of the master's commands.

Understanding the use of a yoke expands the meaning of Jesus' request to be yoked with Him. He wants to bear our burdens, so we are not carrying the weight of it all. Jesus wants to share His strength, so that we can rely on Him every day, not just when life gets difficult or we get weary. He wants to teach us how to follow the Father's commands, how to walk faithfully in this life while listening to His voice. Jesus wants to do the heavy lifting while we **learn from Him**—which is the third thing He asks of us in the Matthew verses above.

In the Old Testament, God uses an interesting phrase to describe His people from time to time. When they were moving away from Him, lacking trust and seeking their own way, He called them "stiff-necked". (See Deuteronomy 9:13 or 2 Chronicles 30:8 NIV for examples.) The meaning of this phrase relates to the yoke, as a stiff-necked animal is one that resists the yoke. God saw that His people were resistant to His yoke.

Don't forget that Jesus called His yoke *easy*. He plans to do the heavy lifting. The advantage here is that we can find rest, even amidst uphill battles and heavy burdens. Rest comes when we let God do the hard work as we trust in Him. Yes, we are often required to work hard, to sacrifice, and to stand firm when things are difficult. But God knows that we cannot do that on our own. That's why Jesus shares His yoke with us—to provide the spiritual and emotional rest that we need.

Over the past couple of years, I have been learning the value of spiritual rest... mostly at 3:00 AM when I have woken up to find myself on the hamster wheel of worry and anxiety. The thoughts that run through my head in the night watches fall into two categories: (1) thoughts of shame regarding things I have done, or (2) thoughts about immediate or future circumstances that I have no control over. I can easily be up for an hour or more, trying to wrestle these thoughts to the ground in order to go back to sleep. What I've been learning to do is to recognize right then that I am not alone. I am yoked with Jesus, who helps me see the truth regarding the troublesome thoughts. He is well in control of everything, and I can go back to sleeping in peace.

Return to your rest, my soul, for the Lord has been good to you. Psalm 116:7

Like the psalmist, we must tell our souls to rest. Jesus is in the driver's seat of the yoke we share, and He will always be good to us. Once we get to that place of trust, we can rest. The truth is that *we will not experience true physical rest unless we are experiencing spiritual rest.*

❦ How are you feeling about being yoked with Jesus? Talk to Him about it.

❦ Pray through the verses from Matthew 11 at the beginning of today's devotion. Listen for any encouragement that the Lord may give you during or after your prayer.

Day 14: Restoration

He restores my soul. He leads me in paths of righteousness
for his name's sake. {Psalm 23:3}

We've come to my favorite line in the entire psalm: *He restores my soul.* In my initial readings, the phrase did not stand out, but once I explored the layers of meaning for the word *restore*, God really began to speak.

🌀 What does *restoring your soul* mean to you?

The most common definition of restore is *to return something to its original state*, which sums up what most people think about God restoring or refreshing their souls. However, take a moment to think about what it means when a car or a piece of furniture is being restored. During the restoration process, when the item is being returned to its original state, it goes through repair and renovation. Old layers must be stripped down and vital parts are often taken apart to be cleaned and reassembled. Consider this as it applies to our souls. God is faithful to repair and renovate our souls when we have gone through hard seasons of loss, rebellion, betrayal, doubt, wandering and more. I am getting a mental picture of the Lord busy at work, repairing our hearts and souls, as we lay still under His skillful and healing hands.

🌀 What comes to mind as you think about this definition of *restore*?

To restore also means *to bring back or reinstate.* This adds another layer of meaning to God's restoration process. I can think of many times in my life when Jesus sought to catch me and bring me back to where I belong... back to the pasture and still waters. Back to His presence. Back to the yoke, sharing the burden, with Jesus in the driver's seat. Back to a place of rest.

❀ How has the Lord recently brought you back to where you needed to be?

As if we haven't heard enough, restoration also means *to give something that was stolen or lost back to the original owner.*[4] This definition reminds me of the parable that Jesus told about a wandering sheep:

For the Son of Man has come to save that which was lost. What do you think? If a man has a hundred sheep, and one of them goes astray, does he not leave the ninety-nine and go to the mountains to seek the one that is straying? And if he should find it, assuredly, I say to you, he rejoices more over that sheep than over the ninety-nine that did not go astray. Matthew 18:11-13

Restoring our souls is a work that Jesus has whole-heartedly committed to. He knows that it will be necessary from time to time! Notice that this sheep was already in the fold. It seems to me that Jesus is not talking about a lost sheep that is made into a new convert, but about believers like you and me. Also notice that the shepherd rejoices over the sheep when it is found and restored to him. Often when we have wandered, run, made our own way, or hidden from the Lord, we beat ourselves up about it. There is no criticism of the sheep in these verses. Jesus knows that sheep wander, get lost and stolen, and He is willing to leave the ninety-nine to come and restore us back to where we belong. He's ready to do it as many times as we need.

🌀 Which definition of restore on pages 45-46 (in italics) speaks to you the most?

🌀 In what way do you need to be restored? Talk to Jesus about that now.

Day 15: Downcast Sheep

He restores my soul. He leads me in paths of righteousness
for his name's sake. {Psalm 23:3}

Have you ever heard of a downcast sheep? Shepherds must often help sheep that have been stranded upside down on their backs in the pasture. This happens when the animal's equilibrium gets out of balance due to heavy fleece or pregnancy, and unfortunately their body structure makes it impossible for downcast sheep to right themselves. Being downcast is quite dangerous. Sheep can die of suffocation within hours of falling and landing on their backs due to gas buildup in their abdomens.

Shepherds must find the downcast sheep in time and help the creature up. Because of circulation and breathing trouble, the shepherd must hold the sheep upright for a few minutes until the animal is restored upright again.[5] Some scholars believe that this process may have been what David was referring to when he wrote *He restores my soul*.

This predicament paints a vivid picture of how you and I can get out of balance and fall into places that we can't get out of. Our Shepherd finds us, picks us up, and restores us to our feet again.

The longer I live, the more I realize how powerless we are over the people and circumstances of our lives. The powerlessness we face when our loved ones are broken, when injustice reigns, or when provision and dreams seem out of reach is so painful! We are much like a sheep on its back in the pasture, unable to control the things that mean the most to us. However, while we lie on our backs, we realize what IS in our power to do: PRAY and TRUST.

When we are stuck in the shame of past events or failures, He sets us upright with the truth of who we are in Him. When we run ahead to the future, running scenarios in our heads, He brings us back to the present, where He is sovereign over everything. When we land upside down in the middle of someone else's mess, trying to fix everything, He puts us back on our feet in our own pasture. When we are on our backs, legs flailing, desperately trying to manage circumstances that are out of our control, He reminds us that He is in control.

The word *downcast* may seem familiar to you because it's found quite a few times in Scripture. Some Bible versions have translated the word as *cast down*, or other adjectives like *dejected*. Here is an example from Lamentations that reminds us how the Lord responds when we are downcast:

I remember my affliction and my wandering, the bitterness and the gall. I well remember them, and my soul is downcast within me. Yet this I call to mind and therefore I have hope: Because of the Lord's great love we are not consumed, for his compassions never fail. They are new every morning; great is your faithfulness. Lamentations 3: 19-23

꙲ How have you felt downcast in the past, and how did the Shepherd set you back on your feet?

꙲ Are you feeling downcast right now? Share your heart with the Lord and ask Him to restore you.

Day 16: The Shepherd's Paths

He restores my soul. He leads me in paths of righteousness
for his name's sake. {Psalm 23:3}

Since sheep are wandering creatures, shepherds have their work cut out for them when it comes to leading the flock. Fortunately, sheep can be trained to distinguish and rely on the voice of their shepherd to lead them. Jesus talked about this in the gospel of John.

Very truly I tell you... The one who enters by the gate is the
shepherd of the sheep. The gatekeeper opens the gate for him,
and the sheep listen to his voice. He calls his own sheep by
name and leads them out. When he has brought out all his
own, he goes on ahead of them, and his sheep follow him be-
cause they know his voice. But they will never follow a
stranger; in fact, they will run away from him because they do
not recognize a stranger's voice. John 10:1-5

As our Shepherd, Jesus will lead us on *paths of righteousness* if we can learn to listen to His voice. Making decisions about which path to take is probably the area of my life that God first used in order to teach me to be more dependent on Him. As a recovering perfectionist, I tend to put an incredible amount of pressure on myself to choose correctly when making big decisions. For the first half of my Christian life, I would often pray about these decisions, but then I would proceed to analyze and strategize in my own mind rather than press into the Lord for His answer.

Years ago, when I was leading a ministry for moms, the pressure to make the right decisions and stay on the path He was choosing became greater. There were two hundred people counting on me to lead well and choose wisely. God allowed the pressure of leadership to build until I could not bear it on my own anymore. The scales tipped and I was finally more concerned about doing things His way than having to analyze everything and figure out the answer on my own. For the first time, I began to consistently call out to Him for wisdom and guidance, and He gave it, as promised in the following passage.

I will instruct you and teach you in the way you should go; I will counsel you with my loving eye on you. Do not be like the horse or the mule, which have no understanding but must be controlled by bit and bridle or they will not come to you. Many are the woes of the wicked, but the Lord's unfailing love surrounds the one who trusts in him. Psalm 32:8-10

God says that He will do more than just guide us: He will instruct, teach, and counsel us. He is present in our circumstances and wants to lead us in a very personal and loving way. Here we see a veiled comparison between sheep and other animals. While sheep can be trained to follow their shepherd's voice, some animals lack the understanding and willingness to come when called. In this case, a bit and bridle must be used to get the animal to come along. God encourages us to be more like sheep, trusting in the Shepherd and following when called. When we don't, He will use something as a bit and bridle to steer us along. In my life, He has used illness, conflict, financial trouble, closed doors, and many other things as a bridle to get my attention and draw me back to Himself.

The truth is that He often leads us where we don't want to go— but for good reason. Shepherds know that their sheep need to be rotated to different pastures to avoid overgrazing and depleting the land. Sheep will stay in one familiar place for too long without the guidance of a good shepherd. A flock can chew the grass of a pasture down to nothing and even destroy the roots. In that case, a pasture will not be available for future grazing.

Perhaps you have been moved to another pasture or led down a hard path for reasons you cannot understand. Trust the Shepherd's perspective, which is so much broader and wiser than your own. Maybe you are struggling to lay down your own decision-making processes. We cannot continue to do things our own way and tack on a prayer at the beginning or the end. We are called to be sheep that follow the Shepherd's voice, letting go of the need to analyze and control the path of our lives.

🌀 Has the Shepherd ever moved you from somewhere before you were willing to go? How did it turn out?

🌀 Think about how generous and caring the Shepherd has appeared in our readings so far. Is He worthy of your full trust?

🌀 Talk to Him about your desire to trust Him and the obstacles that are getting in the way.

Day 17: For the Shepherd's Glory

He restores my soul. He leads me in paths of righteousness for his name's sake. {Psalm 23:3}

David writes that the purpose for the righteous paths the Shepherd leads us on is for His name's sake. Another way to put this is *for His glory*. This is something for us to keep in mind when God leads us down a new or unfamiliar path that we don't understand or agree with. Ultimately, the Lord wants to make His name known to every person He has created. The work He does in us, and the paths He leads us on, will further His reputation and bring Him glory. Let's look at some quotes from Jesus and what He said about the Father's name sake—the Father's glory.

I am the vine; you are the branches. If you remain in me and I in you, you will bear much fruit; apart from me you can do nothing... This is to my Father's glory, that you bear much fruit, showing yourselves to be my disciples.   John 15:5,8

Here we learn that believers bring glory to God when they bear fruit. When I think about a fruit tree, the fruit is both the *primary identifying factor* of the tree (an apple tree bears apples) and the *evidence* of its health and productivity. The fruit that the Holy Spirit bears in and through us (Galatians 5:22-23) both identifies us as believers and is the evidence that He at work in us. It makes sense that something so visible would bring glory to Him. We can be sure that the Shepherd is going to lead us down paths that will bear fruit and glorify Him.

Jesus (speaking about Lazarus' illness) said, "This sickness will not end in death. No, it is for God's glory so that God's Son

may be glorified through it." John 11:4   (If you are not familiar
with the story of Lazarus, read John 11:1-44)

These words from Jesus reveal that suffering also brings glory. Lazarus's family suffered great hardship, not only as they watched their loved one struggle with illness and die, but also as they wrestled to understand Jesus' delay and weigh out the value of the present life versus eternal life. That is a heavy load to bear! In the end, Lazarus and his family learned that Jesus is Lord over both life and death, and that the story is never over until Jesus finishes what He intends to do. The paths of righteousness that our Shepherd leads us on will include hardships, delays, and suffering. He does this because He knows what is at the end of the path of hardship—the incredible demonstration of God's glory.

Several years ago, the Lord called me to step in as a temporary leader of one of the ministries at our church. I questioned the Lord about what He was doing, and why He was doing it, because I felt overwhelmed by all the ministry details and duties, in addition to my already full schedule. As a long-time procrastinator, this ministry assignment quickly became the crucible in which I would either be consumed or purified. The fire became hotter as, for three years, the Lord would not answer my request to be released. Eventually, I began to pray other prayers instead: *Help me to manage my time. Help me to stop coming unraveled on Sunday mornings as I try to get out the door. Help me to serve with joy. Help me to do this well.*

Slowly, the Lord began to show me how to manage my time and responsibilities in a new way. God was very clear about the need to prioritize my to-do list by *time sensitivity* rather than *personal preference*. This may seem like an obvious time management skill, but to me, it was life changing. And apparently, I could not have learned it anywhere else but on this hard path of ministry leadership.

I began to prioritize my days according to the Lord's direction, and things began to shift. I was not crying on Sunday mornings or

56

staying up past midnight on Saturday nights. By the time that the Lord released me from the ministry, I realized the great thing He had done: I wasn't sabotaging myself with procrastination in my everyday life anymore. The fruit from this hard season continues to bless me, and my family, as I serve them in a much healthier and balanced way. I can look back on the experience with joy, knowing that God delivered me from something that was sucking the life out of me and I give Him all the glory!

It's one thing to follow our Shepherd because we agree with where He's leading, but it's entirely another thing to follow Him on paths that we don't want to go down. That requires more faith and trust. We must keep in mind that whether a path leads to suffering or not, it will definitely lead to fruit and glory. We must ask the Lord to give us the willingness to lay down our perspectives and preferences, and to continue following Him wherever He leads.

🌀 Can you think of a time that God led you down a path of hardship that resulted in a display of fruit and glory?

🌀 Are you struggling to accept the path that God has led or is leading you on right now? Talk openly with the Lord about it. Listen for any answers or insight that He may give to boost your trust in Him.

Day 18: Listen to the Song of the Shepherd

We are halfway through the verses of Psalm 23, and it's a good time to stop and read through the entire passage again.

The Lord is my shepherd, I shall not want.

He makes me lie down in green pastures,

He leads me beside quiet waters,

He restores my soul.

He guides me in paths of righteousness for His name's sake.

Even though I walk through the valley of the shadow of death,

I fear no evil, for You are with me.

Your rod and Your staff, they comfort me.

You prepare a table before me in the presence of my enemies.

You have anointed my head with oil; my cup overflows.

Surely goodness and lovingkindness (mercy) will follow me

all the days of my life,

and I will dwell in the house of the Lord forever.

Psalm 23, NASB

Take some time to answer the following questions.

֍ What is the main thing the Lord has shown you so far on our journey through the Shepherd's Psalm?

֍ Read the psalm again, but this time, allow the Lord to read the verses to you through the Holy Spirit's voice in your mind. Allow Him to change any pronouns or words as He reads to you. This might seem unorthodox, but I challenge you to give it a try! Record any insights or words of encouragement that you receive.

֍ What is He calling or inviting you to today?

Day 19: In the Valley

Even though I walk through the valley of the shadow of death, I fear no evil, for you are with me. {Psalm 23:4}

Shepherds in ancient Palestine often led their sheep to mountain terrain in the summer for cooler temperatures and new water sources that hadn't dried up in the summer heat. They also did this to let the lower pastures rest and regrow while the flock fed on alpine meadows.[6] It was quite precarious to lead the sheep through the mountain valleys, along precipices and ledges. We can imagine that some valleys were cast in dark shadows even during the daytime, when the valley walls blocked natural sunlight. During these dark and dangerous times, it was even more critical for sheep to stay near the shepherd and follow his voice.

It's interesting that David's pronouns shift at this point in the psalm. In the first three verses, he talks about his Shepherd using the pronoun *He*, but now shifts to addressing the Lord more directly and personally as *You*. As David writes about *the valley of the shadow of death*, he feels the need to draw closer to the Lord.

We know that dark valleys are a part of this life. After all, Jesus told us in John 16:33 that living in the world as we do, we will encounter trouble especially if we are following in His footsteps. Jesus faced all kinds of opposition and trouble, including being arrested, standing trial, and being sentenced to death.

Based on the anguish He experienced while praying in the garden of Gethsemane, we can assume that the hardest thing He had to do was to lay down His own life.

They went to a place called Gethsemane, and Jesus said to his disciples, "Sit here while I pray." He took Peter, James and John along with him, and he began to be deeply distressed and

61

troubled. *"My soul is overwhelmed with sorrow to the point of death,"* he said to them. *"Stay here and keep watch."*

Going a little farther, he fell to the ground and prayed that, if possible, the hour might pass from him. "Abba, Father," he said, "everything is possible for you. Take this cup from me. Yet not what I will, but what you will." Mark 14:32-36

It seems that the most difficult thing Jesus had to do on this earth was to surrender His own will and submit to the Father's will, knowing it would cost Him everything. This was Jesus' darkest valley, but He knew the value of what God was asking Him to do.

Jesus replied, "The hour has come for the Son of Man to be glorified. Very truly I tell you, unless a kernel of wheat falls to the ground and dies, it remains only a single seed. But if it dies, it produces many seeds." John 12:23-25

Jesus saw Himself as a seed willing to fall to the ground and die to produce great fruit—the salvation of all mankind. Perhaps our darkest valleys also come when we are asked to lay down and die to ourselves.

Whoever wants to be my disciple must deny themselves and take up their cross and follow me. For whoever wants to save their life will lose it, but whoever loses their life for me and for the gospel will save it. What good is it for someone to gain the whole world, yet forfeit their soul? Mark 8:34-36

When we are willing to deny ourselves or die to ourselves, we are split open like the seed that Jesus talked about in John 12:24, and fruit results. The Shepherd's paths for us will include dark valleys that require us to die to ourselves in some manner. Could it be that David's *valley of the shadow of death* is really *the valley of the shadow of dying to self*?

Perhaps we will give up or lose something dear, walk through illness or disability, or be required to put someone else before ourselves in an extreme way. Perhaps we will not be able to save the one we love, or we will have to let go of a dream that is precious to us.

Laying down my life and my will the way that Jesus did in the garden usually requires recognizing my complete powerlessness over the situation. Jesus recognized that He wasn't in charge of the cup He would drink. He knew He would not be able to persuade the Father to change His will. When we find ourselves in this position, all we can do is call out to God and pray what Jesus prayed: *Not my will, but Yours be done.*

This is the valley of the shadow of death to self. You will walk it, but you will not walk it alone. Jesus, the one who walked it before you, will be with you all the way. He will be your light in the darkness. He will be the power behind your yes—your willingness to lay down your life and your will. He will be the Shepherd that leads and feeds you in the valley. And he will be the one who leads you out when it is over.

🌀 Reflect on a dark valley from the past. How was Jesus present there with you? If you're not sure, ask Him to show you where He was.

🌀 What good came out of that dark valley that you went through?

🌀 Talk to God about any valleys you are currently facing, or sense may be coming. Remember Jesus' honesty in His garden prayer? Don't hold anything back. Share all that is on your heart and then listen for His reply.

Day 20: Fearing No Evil

Even though I walk through the valley of the shadow of death, I fear no evil, for you are with me. {Psalm 23:4}

Fear is a natural response to darkness, trouble, and death. David knew this as he wrote the words above. His ability to *fear no evil* did not come from his courage, but from awareness of the Shepherd's close presence. We are not required to talk ourselves out of fear. We are encouraged to draw close to God, which pushes the fear away.

There is no fear in love. But perfect love drives out fear, because fear has to do with punishment. The one who fears is not made perfect in love. 1 John 4:18

🌀 What do you fear most?

🌀 How does God's love ease your fear?

Having someone close by makes such a big difference in our level of fear. Think about noises in the middle of the night, driving on dark and unfamiliar roads, or going to serious doctor appointments. Having someone with us, holding our hand or offering words of encouragement can make all the difference.

Sometimes we forget that we are NEVER alone. Even if there are no other people with us, Jesus is always with us.

This is what the Lord says—he who created you, Jacob, he who formed you, Israel: "Do not fear, for I have redeemed you; I have summoned you by name; you are mine. When you pass through the waters, I will be with you; when you pass through the rivers, they will not sweep over you. When you walk through the fire, you will not be burned; the flames will not set you ablaze. For I am the Lord your God, the Holy One of Israel, your Savior... Since you are precious and honored in my sight, and because I love you, I will give people in exchange for you, nations in exchange for your life. Do not be afraid, for I am with you." Isaiah 43:1-5a

Our Shepherd promises to be with us in every circumstance, no matter how difficult. In the waters, he will buoy us up so that we will not go under. In the fire, He will stand between us and the flames so that we are not burned. In the dark valleys, He will guide us and carry us through.

We fear things like snakes and rats and heights, but we also fear things like rejection, failure, and missing out on opportunities. However, the things many of us fear most are probably the future scenarios we make up in our minds! These are perceived threats rather than real threats. What if, instead of running *worst-case scenarios* in our heads, we ran *best-case scenarios*? What if we imagined Jesus there with us in those future situations? What if we ran scenarios that included Him there in person, right next to us? Think about that for a minute.

About a year ago, I was working with a therapist to resolve some memories of abuse from my childhood. We used a mode of therapy called EMDR, which works to separate the intense emotions that are attached to traumatic memories. It allows the brain to store the memories differently, significantly reducing the pain associated with the memory.

66

An upcoming appointment was giving me anxiety because I knew we were going to work through a very specific and powerful memory. I felt physically ill the morning of the appointment because I did not want to relive that moment from the past. When I arrived at the therapist's office, I confessed all my anxiety, but told her that I wanted to face it so that I could move on.

As soon as we began and my mind took me back in time, I was relieved to see Jesus standing right next to me in that memory. I actually felt embarrassed, because I had forgotten that Jesus always appeared in the memories we worked through. *My anxiety had caused me to forget that He is ALWAYS with me.* On this particular day, the resolution of the memory I feared turned out to be the most amazing experience I'd had in my therapy. His presence brought the peace that surpasses understanding and the healing that set me free.

🌀 What are you feeling anxious or fearful about today?

🌀 How aware are you of His close presence at this moment? Close your eyes and imagine Jesus sitting next to you. Let Him minister to you.

🌀 Write down any insights you'd like to remember.

Day 21: The Shepherd's Rod

I fear no evil, for you are with me. Your rod and Your staff comfort me. {Psalm 23:4}

The shepherds of David's time had two tools that they kept handy: the rod and the staff. Today we will focus on the first. The shepherd's rod was like a wooden club, narrow on one end for gripping, and rounded on the other end. This tool had several uses in the working life of a shepherd as he cared for his sheep.

A shepherd would periodically gather his flock into an enclosed area while he stood at the entrance. The sheep would pass one at a time under his rod for inspection and counting. The rod was used to separate the sheep's wool, exposing the skin underneath, which could be checked for health issues or wounds.[7] This use of the rod shows the shepherd's great care for his flock.

The rod was also used as a weapon to protect the sheep. Shepherds today would likely use a rifle to stop predators from attacking the flock, but ancient shepherds used the rod to strike any threat close at hand or hurled it at predators that were out of arm's reach.

Lastly, the rod was used as a means of discipline among the sheep. Members of the flock would sometimes need a nudge with the rod to head in the right direction or stay out of something harmful. All training and discipline from the shepherd was for the flock's own good, for each one's safety. Hebrews 12 shows very clearly what our Shepherd's motivation is regarding discipline:

Have you completely forgotten this word of encouragement that addresses you as a father addresses his son? It says (in Proverbs 3:11-12),

"My son, do not make light of the Lord's discipline, and do not lose heart when He rebukes you, because the Lord disciplines the one he loves, and he chastens everyone he accepts as his son."

Endure hardship as discipline; God is treating you as his children. For what children are not disciplined by their father? If you are not disciplined—and everyone undergoes discipline— then you are not legitimate, not true sons and daughters at all. Moreover, we have all had human fathers who disciplined us, and we respected them for it. How much more should we submit to the Father of spirits and live! They disciplined us for a little while as they thought best; but God disciplines us for our good, in order that we may share in his holiness. No discipline seems pleasant at the time, but painful. Later on, however, it produces a harvest of righteousness and peace for those who have been trained by it.   *Hebrews 12: 5-11*

David writes in Psalm 23 that the rod is a comfort to him. This caused me to examine my heart. While I find comfort in God's protection and in passing under the Shepherd's rod of care, do I find comfort in His discipline?

Honestly, I have a history of fearing the Lord's discipline. He has revealed the root of this fear, which stems from two main problems: unrealistic expectations and broken filters. Perfectionism causes me to have unrealistic expectations for myself, and I tend to project those on to God as though He expects the same from me. If I am never good enough in my own eyes, I can't possibly be good enough in His eyes. These unrealistic expectations also serve as the broken filter through which I hear God's words when I read the Bible. Truly, I have used Scripture to brow beat myself for many years. With this approach to God and His Word, I was always fearful of the discipline that I thought I deserved.

God has been transforming the way that I hear His voice and read the Bible. He challenges me to read Scripture and hear it through the filter of *His love* rather than *judgment*. I realized that I had been assuming what God would say, and how He would say it to me, rather than truly listening to Him. I had to turn off the internal dialogue of expectations and shame, and tune into what God was trying to communicate to me. What a transformation in my heart, my mind, and my life! It has allowed me to truly see and hear God's love for me. When His correction or discipline comes, it is so much kinder than I imagined it would be.

> *Do you show contempt for the riches of his kindness, forbearance and patience, not realizing that God's kindness is intended to lead you to repentance? Romans 2:4*

God's first attempt at correcting us always comes in a kind manner. He is gentle, wanting us to respond with repentance. When we see His firm or harsh discipline in the Bible, it is typically a last resort after He has tried many other avenues to correct His children.

You can learn to take comfort in His rod of discipline, knowing that it is kind and gentle. When you are not fearful or defensive, your heart is in a much better position to receive His correction. His rod is set on protecting you, nudging you away from harmful things, teaching you a better way.

🌀 Can you relate to fearing God's correction or discipline? If so, what might be the reason?

🌀 Are there any filters affecting the way that you read the Bible or hear God's voice?

🌀 Talk to the Lord about any fears or filters that you sense are getting in the way. Ask Him to remove them so you can hear Him through a filter of love and approval.

Day 22: The Shepherd's Staff

I fear no evil, for you are with me. Your rod and Your staff
comfort me. {Psalm 23:4}

The shepherd's staff was long and slender, with a curved end that looked like a hook. You've likely seen an ancient shepherd leaning on his staff in a nativity set. Usually taller than the shepherd, the highly visible staff identified him and his occupation.

This tool was useful as a walking stick on rough terrain, or for testing the depth of streams and pools. The curved end served to capture or guide sheep that needed to be redirected or brought back to the flock. Sometimes lambs were separated from their mothers and the shepherd used the staff to lead the baby directly back to the ewe.[8] Being quite long, the staff significantly extended the reach of the shepherd, so that he was able to tend to a wide circle within his flock. The sheep were rarely out of the reach of his care.

When it comes to our Shepherd, we are never out of His reach. He always sees us, finds us, rescues us, restores us, returns us where we belong.

Surely the arm of the Lord is not too short to save, nor his ear
too dull to hear. Isaiah 59:1

I waited patiently for the Lord; he turned to me and heard my
cry. He lifted me out of the slimy pit, out of the mud and mire;
he set my feet on a rock and gave me a firm place to stand.
Psalm 40:1-3

The Shepherd's staff is a symbol of His guidance, protection, love, and course correction. We can always count on His gentle nudging and take comfort in the corralling of our wandering hearts and feet.

His staff redirects our course and blocks paths that aren't good for us.

When God first called Moses to lead His people, he was a shepherd tending his father-in-law's sheep in Midian. Moses' shepherding staff became a powerful vehicle for God's power as it was used to initiate the plagues on Egypt and to split the Red Sea (Exodus 14). This simple staff represented God's ability to do the impossible, to bring deliverance in a no-win situation, and to show incredible favor to His children.

The Shepherd staff is a reminder that God can do what is beyond your reach, beyond your abilities, or beyond your power. Our Shepherd can do what is beyond your imagination and expectation. He can do what you can't even imagine to ask for in prayer! His reach exceeds yours every time.

The woman who had bled for more than 12 years was beyond the reach of doctors and cures, yet Jesus had the power to heal her (Mark 5:25-34). The deliverance of a demon possessed boy was beyond the reach of the disciples, who were unable to heal him, but Jesus demonstrated His powerful reach into the spiritual realm and the boy was healed in an instant (Mark 9:17-29).

We will face things in this life that put us out of reach of the world's solutions, cures, and experts. We will face circumstances that put us out beyond the reach of well-meaning loved ones. Do not despair, as alone as you may feel, for the reach of the Shepherd's staff is always wide enough to catch you or to save you.

The enemy has a way of using shame to isolate us and make us feel like we are the ONE that is too far gone, too broken, or too troublesome. I'll refresh your memory regarding our reading on day 14 and Jesus's willingness to leave the ninety-nine to go after the one. *You are the one!* The one He loves, the one He wants, the one He is ready to rescue no matter the circumstances. And do not forget that He rejoices over the one that is rescued. He rejoices over you!

🌀 Recall a time when you felt the reach of the Lord's arm to help you. Spend some time thanking Him for that.

🌀 What feels out of your reach today? Recognize that this situation is not out of God's reach. Find comfort in the Shepherd's staff and His ability to do the impossible and the unexpected.

Day 23: The Shepherd's Table

You prepare a table before me in the presence of my enemies. {Psalm 23:5}

Scholars have wondered and debated whether David deviated from the shepherd theme when he wrote verse five. It's here that the imagery changes from the pasture and sheep to a banquet table.

One could argue that the imagery hasn't changed that much. The pasture is a kind of table for the flock, as it's where they gather and eat. The shepherd prepares the table by choosing ample pastures and leading the flock to feast there.

Consider Jesus, who gathered His flock of thousands on grassy hills to hear His teachings and enjoy a miraculous lunch. It was there that the Lord hosted a banquet in a pasture:

> *"Bring them here to me," Jesus said. And he directed the people to sit down on the grass. Taking the five loaves and the two fish and looking up to heaven, he gave thanks and broke the loaves. Then he gave them to the disciples, and the disciples gave them to the people. They all ate and were satisfied, and the disciples picked up twelve basketfuls of broken pieces that were left over. The number of those who ate was about five thousand men, besides women and children. Matthew 14:18-21*

The table that the Lord prepares for us is wherever He invites us and provides for us. The table He has prepared for you may be set in the most unusual time or place, but it will be the ideal time and place.

🌀 What comes to your mind as you think about the Lord preparing a table for you?

It's an interesting thought to imagine God preparing a table for us. We are so often in servant mode, that we don't think about God serving us. The word *prepare* in the original language means *to furnish, arrange, set in order*. Preparation gives the implication of an invitation, and the table indicates a meal. The Shepherd has offered us the opportunity to come and dine with Him. His preparation and invitation impart to us great dignity as His guest. The question is whether we will come and sit with Him.

I'm reminded of the story of dinner at Mary and Martha's house in Luke 10. As you read, observe the interactions through the lens of the Shepherd's invitation to His table.

As Jesus and his disciples were on their way, he came to a village where a woman named Martha opened her home to him. She had a sister called Mary, who sat at the Lord's feet listening to what he said. But Martha was distracted by all the preparations that had to be made. She came to him and asked, "Lord, don't you care that my sister has left me to do the work by myself? Tell her to help me!"

"Martha, Martha," the Lord answered, "you are worried and upset about many things, but few things are needed— indeed only one. Mary has chosen what is better, and it will not be taken away from her." Luke 10:38-42

This is a passage that has been dissected over and over in the church, sometimes taking a critical view of Martha. I'm not here to give Martha a hard time; she felt both called and honored to host Jesus in her home. I'm just wondering if Mary felt called in a different way. Perhaps she heard the Shepherd's invitation to come to His table, and she simply obeyed that call.

Are we more comfortable in the Martha role, busy with preparation, service, or hosting duties? Are we less comfortable heeding the Lord's invitation to come and simply sit with Him? Certainly, there is a time for both. However, there is often more vulnerability required when one is a guest at His table. Some might find it easy to run and evade transparency with Him in the doing and serving and preparing, but the invitation stands. Come and sit with Me.

🌀 Today, you are invited to His table. Will you come and stay a while?

🌀 What do you hope to find on this table?

🌀 Take a few minutes to close your eyes, imagining the banquet He has prepared for you. It might be in a grand hall, in a quiet cozy corner with a cup of tea, or out in the landscape of His creation. Imagine yourself seated with Jesus. Let Him speak first. Record any details or insights you want to remember.

Day 24: In the Presence of My Enemies

You prepare a table before me in the presence of my enemies. {Psalm 23:5}

Shepherds have always been required to assess the threat of nearby predators and thieves that would do harm to the flock. Every time he leads his sheep to feed in the pasture, he knows that an enemy could be close. He lets the flock graze while he keeps watch.

The phrase *in the presence of my enemies* is actually one verb in the original Hebrew. It means *to bind or tie up, to make narrow a passage, to cause distress, to press hard upon, to vex, show hostility*. With this insight, verse five could be translated as:

You prepare a table before me while the enemy besieges me.

Our Shepherd knows that the enemy will always be stalking about, looking for an opportunity to steal and destroy. Not only does God provide a table for us that draws us in and meets our needs, He does this in full view of the enemy. Satan sees all that we are given, all that we are waiting for, all that God has done in us, all that is left to do. He sees our gifts, our calling, our purpose. We might have seasons of being hidden from others, but we are not hidden from the enemy.

The result of this arrangement is that Satan will always come against us to steal the word of promise or the word of encouragement that God has given us. When we have been promised victory or provision, he will often come to steal our assurance and attempt to weaken our faith.

Listen! A farmer went out to sow his seed. As he was scattering the seed, some fell along the path, and the birds came and ate it up. Mark 4: 3-4

81

(Jesus explained the meaning of the story)...The farmer sows the word. Some people are like seed along the path, where the word is sown. As soon as they hear it, Satan comes and takes away the word that was sown in them. Mark 4:14-15

During the season of financial hardship that I wrote about earlier in this book, God called me to do two things that didn't seem to make sense. The first was having a baby, and the second was homeschooling our two daughters. I wrestled these things out with God, thinking surely it wasn't time for a baby, and certainly I should have looked for a job to try to make ends meet instead of homeschooling. Over and over, the Lord was clear about where He wanted me.

On more than one occasion, my husband and I faced heavy criticism from other Christians for the choices we were making. The very things God commanded us to do were the exact points of attack from the enemy. He came to snatch away the word God had given us. The fact that the enemy used fellow believers made it more painful, but we did our best to stand on what the Lord had already confirmed multiple times.

🌀 How has the enemy come against you recently?

Despite the resistance you are experiencing, despite the fiery arrows of the enemy, you have a place at the Lord's table. You still have ample provision for what you need today. He provides abundantly to cover what the enemy will steal from your table.

Only do not let the enemy keep you from the Lord's table. He will try everything in his power to keep you from being nourished and encouraged by your Shepherd. Satan will lie to you, accuse you, and try to disqualify you from taking your seat at the table.

❀ Has the enemy been trying to keep you from the Lord's table? Ask God to make you increasingly hungry for His word and His presence so that you will not be deterred from coming.

❀ Talk to the Lord about how the enemy is pressing hard upon you. Listen for His comfort and guidance.

Day 25: The Shepherd's Healing Touch

You anoint my head with oil; my cup overflows. {Psalm 23:5}

Shepherds in biblical times used oil for the healing of wounds and to refresh the skin of both man and beast in a very dry climate. A mixture of olive oil, sulfur and spices served to repel insects that were attracted to the creature's eyes and nose. The mixture also served as protection against skin conditions caused by parasites.[9]

The anointing that David mentions in verse five illustrates a shepherd's attentive care for the health of his sheep. The anointing was intended for both protection and for healing. Remember in Ezekiel 34 when God criticized the spiritual shepherds of His people for their lack of care?

You have not strengthened the weak or healed the sick or bound up the injured. You have not brought back the strays or searched for the lost. You have ruled them harshly and bru-tally. Ezek. 34:4

You'll recall that God follows the criticism of these shepherds with the promise to administer the very tenderest care for His flock Himself. He also promised, through the prophet Isaiah, that Jesus too would minister to the weak, the sick, and the wounded when He came.

He took up our pain and bore our suffering, yet we considered him punished by God, stricken by him, and afflicted. But he was pierced for our transgressions, he was crushed for our in-iquities; the punishment that brought us peace was on him, and by his wounds we are healed. We all, like sheep, have gone astray, each of us has turned to our own way; and the Lord has laid on him the iniquity of us all.   Isaiah 53:4-6

🌀 We can see all kinds of healing promised in this Isaiah passage: physical, emotional, and spiritual. We have a Shepherd that makes tender care and healing a priority. What speaks to you most in the Scripture passages above?

🌀 What kind of healing are you in need of right now? Ask the Shepherd to minister to you with His healing and anointing.

Day 26:   The Shepherd's Anointing

You anoint my head with oil; my cup overflows. {Psalm 23:5}

In addition to his boyhood experiences using oil to tend to his father's sheep, David must have been thinking about his own personal anointing, that the Lord orchestrated through Samuel, when He wrote verse five above.

(God speaking to Samuel) "Fill your horn with oil and be on your way; I am sending you to Jesse of Bethlehem. I have chosen one of his sons to be king."

Jesse had seven of his sons pass before Samuel, but Samuel said to him, "The Lord has not chosen these." He asked Jesse, "Are these all the sons you have?"

"There is still the youngest," Jesse answered. "He is tending the sheep."

Samuel said, "Send for him; we will not sit down until he arrives." So he sent for him and had him brought in. David was glowing with health and had a fine appearance and handsome features.

Then the Lord said, "Rise and anoint him; this is the one." So Samuel took the horn of oil and anointed him in the presence of his brothers, and from that day on the Spirit of the Lord came powerfully upon David. 1 Samuel 16:1b,10-13

It was common practice in the Old Testament to use anointing oil to consecrate priests, as well as important items in the tabernacle or temple. Anointing was also important to confirm a person's calling to leadership or ministry. We see this with prophets, priests and kings in Scripture. The oil that Samuel used to anoint David was specifically made for the occasion, but it had no power of its own. It was symbolic of God's power and favor poured out in the life of David through the Holy Spirit.

Jesus speaks about His own anointing and calling while in a synagogue in Nazareth on the Sabbath (Luke 4). The scheduled reading from the Hebrew scriptures that day was Isaiah 61, which Jesus boldly claimed was prophecy being fulfilled in Him that very day.

The Spirit of the Sovereign Lord is on me because the Lord has anointed me to proclaim good news to the poor. He has sent me to bind up the brokenhearted, to proclaim freedom for the captives and release from darkness for the prisoners, to proclaim the year of the Lord's favor and the day of vengeance of our God, to comfort all who mourn, and provide for those who grieve in Zion— to bestow on them a crown of beauty instead of ashes, the oil of joy instead of mourning, and a garment of praise instead of a spirit of despair. Isaiah 61:1-3

Jesus recognized that the power behind anointing is the Holy Spirit. As the Son of God, He did not venture to live out what God had called Him to do in His own power. Not that Jesus was without power, but I believe that He purposely modeled a Spirit-filled and anointed life to be an example to us. We are not able to live out what God has called us to without the anointing of the Holy Spirit.

Now it is God who makes both us and you stand firm in Christ. He anointed us, set his seal (mark) of ownership on us, and put his Spirit in our hearts as a deposit, guaranteeing what is to come. 2 Corinthians 1:21–22

For the first half of my Christian life, I operated under the assumption that whatever God suggested in Scripture or spoke to my heart was an assignment that I was to go and accomplish, then report back to Him. Of course, I was doing most of these things in my own power. It wasn't until I had been teaching God's Word for some time and first experienced the Holy Spirit's powerful intervention, that I began to understand the power of anointing. One time in the middle of teaching, words and truth that were not in my notes, nor in my previous understanding, began flowing out of my mouth. What a difference the anointing made, compared to teaching or doing some service in my own strength.

Have you ever tried to do something that you strongly felt God calling you to do, but it failed miserably, or limped along without any real life in it? I've had this experience many times, even after experiencing the power of the Holy Spirit's anointing. While the Lord has placed spiritual gifts in us, they do not function properly without the anointing power of the Spirit. There is also a yielding required on our part to fully activate or release the anointing. It's easy to charge forth when we feel called or anointed for something, but **the yielding is essential**. Again, we find that dependence on the Shepherd is key!

🌀 What do you think God's primary calling or purpose for your life is? How is that playing out in your life right now? (It's okay if you don't know the answer to that question! Ask the Lord for guidance and clarity.)

🌀 Have you consciously recognized God's anointing on you to carry out this calling or purpose?

🌀 Take some time to pray about the anointing on your life. Do you need more power? More awareness of the anointing? More guidance? Talk to the Lord about it.

Day 27: The Shepherd's Overflow

You anoint my head with oil; my cup overflows. {Psalm 23:5}

The Bible uses the imagery of a cup to represent both our lives and our fate. David recognized that his cup was full—and that the Lord's anointing on his life through the power of the Holy Spirit was what caused his cup to overflow. This fullness comes because of the constant indwelling and refilling of the Spirit within believers. Think of how many times you fill your coffee mug or water cup in a day. We need repeated refilling like that.

I love that God chose such a small vessel to represent our lives. A cup does not hold much compared to a bowl, pot, pitcher, or tub. A cup holds enough for the moment, and then we must lean back to His table for a new filling from the Lord. The beauty of an often-filled cup is that it won't be stagnant with old contents. It won't be filled with yesterday's anointing or last week's wisdom. We can enjoy a fresh filling meant for the very moment we are facing.

It's important to recognize that the overflow of the cup is not waste. As a mom, I tend to view an overflowing cup at my table as a problem. I might see it as foolishness, as waste or as a mess, but the Lord's overflowing presence in our lives is not a mess. It is never wasted. The overflow is meant for the people around us. When our cups are filled to the brim, we can share with others.

There are seasons in our lives when we may feel like we are being poured out. Perhaps you are feeling like the apostle Paul when his circumstances and responsibilities were weighing heavy on him.

But even if I am being poured out like a drink offering on the sacrifice and service coming from your faith, I am glad and rejoice with you. Philippians. 2:17

91

Paul was able to rejoice in being emptied out, knowing that the Lord was at work in His midst. He knew that being poured out was not the end of the story, but that God would refill him and bless him for being a willing vessel in His hand.

Maybe you are looking at your cup and comparing it to someone else's. Speaking from experience, this is a practice that will empty your cup immediately. Know that God has provisions, insights, opportunities, and blessings that are for no one else but you. All the things that fall inside of your cup are carefully ordained by the Lord, and everything that falls outside of your cup is just as carefully selected.

Lord, you alone are my portion and my cup; you make my lot secure. The boundary lines have fallen for me in pleasant places; surely I have a delightful inheritance. I will praise the Lord, who counsels me; even at night my heart instructs me. I keep my eyes always on the Lord. With him at my right hand, I will not be shaken. Psalm 16:5-8

We must trust the Lord with our portion, and with the places that our boundary lines have fallen. This can be difficult when our cup appears difficult or unlovely or unfair. Even Jesus was required to trust the Father with the choosing of His cup. In tough times, we can follow His example.

Going a little farther, he fell with his face to the ground and prayed, "My Father, if it is possible, may this cup be taken from me. Yet not as I will, but as you will." Matthew 26:39

❀ How is your cup today?

🌀Talk to the Lord about anything you might need. Thank Him for what you find in your cup today.

🌀 Review the verses from Psalm 16 and ask the Lord to read them to you in His voice. Allow Him to personalize the verses and speak directly to your heart.

Day 28: The Shepherd Follows Me

Surely goodness and mercy will follow me all the days of my life, and I will dwell in the house of the Lord forever. {Psalm 23:6}

David begins the closing of his psalm with the assurance that the Shepherd not only leads him, but also follows closely behind him. The omnipresence of God makes this possible. He is simultaneously before you, behind you, beneath you, and beside you.

The Lord himself goes before you and will be with you; he will never leave you nor forsake you. Do not be afraid; do not be discouraged." Deuteronomy 31:8

You hem me in behind and before, and you lay your hand upon me. Psalm 139:5

You will hear a voice behind you saying, "This is the way. Follow it, whether it turns to the right or to the left." Isaiah 30:21

The Lord upholds all who fall and lifts up all who are bowed down. Psalm 145:14

For I am the Lord your God who takes hold of your right hand and says to you, "Do not fear; I will help you." Isaiah 41:13

What does God pursue us *with*? Psalm 23:6 says that He follows us with His *goodness* and *mercy*. He follows us in order to support us, to redirect us, to bless us, and sometimes to bring us back where we belong.

The *goodness* of God is an undisputable fact that, sometimes, can only be seen with eyes of faith. He is good all the time, in every circumstance. He does not know how to do evil. Often when something difficult or tragic comes, we question how God could allow

95

such a thing if He is good. We need eyes of faith to see that His goodness is unchanged in those difficult circumstances.

When I was a young Christian, reading through the Psalms for the first time, I came across what I believed was a typographical error because the language and meaning of the verse did not compute in my brain. I assumed it was a mistake.

It was good for me to be afflicted so that I might learn Your decrees. Psalm 119:71

I could not fathom how being afflicted could ever be a good thing. I had been afflicted, through abuse and abandonment my whole childhood, but I could not see any good in it. I marked the verse with a big "?". Several years later, after the Lord began healing my heart from my affliction, I finally understood. One Sunday morning, when I was volunteering to pray for people after our church service, a woman came forward. By the time she was halfway up the aisle, the Spirit of God impressed on me her story—it was very much like mine. I prayed with her, and while giving her encouragement, the verse in Psalm 119 came back to me. *It was good for me that I had been afflicted*. I found myself feeling grateful for my experience and the healing that the Lord had begun in me, for it qualified me to get on my knees next to another wounded soul and pray for her. It took time and eyes of faith for me to see God's ability to be good and bring good out of my life's affliction.

David also says that God's *mercy* will follow us. All I have to say about that is THANK GOD. I need for the Lord to follow me around with His mercy like one of those white uniformed trash sweepers at Disneyland, cleaning up my messes and mistakes. What a gift His mercy is after we've fallen short in our relationships. What a blessing to know that mercy is the epilogue that follows all our failures. Jesus—thank you.

The Shepherd will follow you all the days of your life. It's true; Psalm 23 says it. He will be right behind you on good days, on hard days, on victorious days, and on bottom-of-the-pit days. He will pursue you with His goodness and His mercy every single day.

🌀 How have you seen His goodness lately?

🌀 How do you need to see His goodness today?

🌀 How do you need His mercy today?

🌀 Meditate or think on the before you, behind you, beneath you, and beside you verses at the beginning of today's writing. Ask the Lord to make you aware of His presence on all sides.

Day 29: In the House of the Lord

Surely goodness and mercy will follow me all the days of my life, and I will dwell in the house of the Lord forever. {Ps 23:6}

Psalm 23 has been so good to us, drawing us closer to the Shepherd. The last phrase here is one that speaks of eternity: *I will dwell in the house of the Lord forever*. To *dwell* means *to stay, to remain, to abide.* Usually, when we go to someone's house, it's for a visit. We don't get to stay more than a meal, a night, or maybe a week. In verse six, however, we are talking about a forever visit, an eternal stay over in the house of the Lord.

The word in the Hebrew used for *house* is the simplest of words for a home. It doesn't mean mansion or palace; it is a simple dwelling. This surprised me. I tend to think of heaven as a vast space with millions upon millions of believers waiting their turn to sit with the Lord. However, this verse gives a different impression, one of sitting in close quarters, enjoying His company and hospitality.

🌀 What does it mean to you to *dwell in the house of the Lord*?

David is confident that he will dwell with the Lord forever. I'm reminded that forever is a time frame that begins now and never ends. Jesus called us to start dwelling and abiding with Him now!

Abide in Me, and I in you. As the branch cannot bear fruit of itself, unless it abides in the vine, neither can you, unless you abide in Me. I am the vine; you are the branches. He who

99

abides in Me, and I in him, bears much fruit; for without Me you can do nothing. If anyone does not abide in Me, he is cast out as a branch and is withered; and they gather them and throw them into the fire, and they are burned. If you abide in Me, and My words abide in you, you will ask what you desire, and it shall be done for you.   John 15:4-7

Notice in the passage above how abiding equals dependence. The branch can produce nothing without the vine. Jesus invites us to abide, knowing that we bring NOTHING to the table except ourselves. That is all He desires. Come, dwell with Him, abide in His love, remain in His presence.

All the imagery God uses in Scripture is so helpful to understand how our relationship with Him works. We are called to a life of abiding in Him, like sheep, totally dependent on the shepherd's care; like a branch, totally dependent on the vine for nourishment and growth; like a guest in the Father's home, totally dependent on His generosity and hospitality. Abiding is not controlling, it is not performing, it is not striving. It is relying on the One who has all the power and provision for our lives.

🌀 What does abiding in Jesus look like to you, in your daily life? Talk to the Lord about your desire to abide in Him more often or more fully. Listen for any encouragement He might give you.

🌀 Take a few minutes to visualize the Lord's house in your mind's eye and imagine what it would be like to be there with Him. Allow the Holy Spirit to guide your imagination. Record any details or insights you would like to remember.

Day 30: Carry the Song of the Shepherd

Here we are at the end of our 30-day journey! I pray that you have been as blessed as I have been in my own journey. Every part of the process has brought new insight, so I am confident that the Lord has brought you new understanding and a deeper experience of the Shepherd's care.

The Lord is my shepherd, I shall not want.

He makes me lie down in green pastures,

He leads me beside quiet waters,

He restores my soul.

He guides me in paths of righteousness for His name's sake.

Even though I walk through the valley of the shadow of death,

I fear no evil, for You are with me.

Your rod and Your staff, they comfort me.

You prepare a table before me in the presence of my enemies.

You have anointed my head with oil; my cup overflows.

Surely goodness and lovingkindness (mercy) will follow me

all the days of my life,

and I will dwell in the house of the Lord forever.

Psalm 23, NASB

🌀 Which phrases speak to you the most? Why?

🌀 How has learning more about sheep and shepherding helped you understand the passage more?

🌀 How has your relationship with the Shepherd deepened?

🌀 What insight from Psalm 23 will you carry forward in your heart?

How can I be saved?

How can I know that I am going to Heaven? Is this really necessary? What does it mean to follow Jesus? You may have many questions, and I will do my best to answer with God's own words from the Bible.

Jesus said, "Very truly I tell you, no one can see the kingdom of God unless they are born again." John 3:3

"All praise to God, the Father of our Lord Jesus Christ. It is by his great mercy that we have been born again, because God raised Jesus Christ from the dead. Now we live with great expectation, and we have a priceless inheritance—an inheritance that is kept in heaven for you, pure and undefiled, beyond the reach of change and decay." 1 Peter 1:3-4 NLT

The book of Romans in the New Testament lays out some clear guidelines regarding being born again and receiving salvation:

It is written: "There is no one righteous, not even one..." Rom 3:10

"...for all have sinned and fall short of the glory of God, and all are justified freely by his grace through the redemption that came by Christ Jesus. God presented Christ as a sacrifice of atonement, through the shedding of his blood—to be received by faith. He did this to demonstrate his righteousness, because in his forbearance he had left the sins committed beforehand unpunished." Romans 3:23-25

"...the wages of sin is death, but the gift of God is eternal life in Christ Jesus our Lord." Romans 6:23

'If you declare with your mouth, "Jesus is Lord," and believe in your heart that God raised him from the dead, you will be saved. For it is with your heart that you believe and are justi- fied, and it is with your mouth that you profess your faith and are saved. As Scripture says, "Anyone who believes in him will never be put to shame...for, "Everyone who calls on the name of the Lord will be saved." Romans 10:9-11, 13

It's clear that God does this work in us, as we can do nothing to save ourselves.

"For it is by grace you have been saved, through faith—and this is not from yourselves, it is the gift of God— not by works, so that no one can boast." Ephesians 2:8-9

I have no doubt that Jesus has used this devotional book to do what He talked about in the following verses:

Jesus said, "Here I am! I stand at the door and knock. If any- one hears my voice and opens the door, I will come in and dine with that person, and they with me. Revelation 3:20

If He is knocking at the door of your heart, I pray that you will let Him in. You can do that easily with a prayer like this:

Jesus, I know that I have sinned and fallen short of both your glory and the person you made me to be. I recognize that you created me, and that You have a plan for my life. Thank you for paying the penalty for my sins by dying on the cross. I ask your forgiveness for all that I've done. I accept the cleansing and grace you have promised to those who believe. Please come in, I am opening the door to my heart and my life. I want you to be my Lord and Savior. Help me to understand all that I am praying and asking. Show me the way from here and help me to find others who can help me grow in my new life with You. Amen.

Endnotes

[1] Wight, Fred K. *Manners and Customs of Bible Lands*. First Edition, Moody Press, Dec. 1953.

[2] Keller, W. Phillip. *A Shepherd Looks at Psalm 23*. Zondervan, 2007, page 42.

[3] "rest." *Lexico Dictionary* powered by Oxford University Press. https://www.lexico.com/en. September 1, 2019.

[4] "restore." *Lexico Dictionary* powered by Oxford University Press. https://www.lexico.com/en. September 14, 2019. All italicized definitions on this page came from lexico.com.

[5] Gulian, Jared. *Getting Intimate with a Cast Sheep*. October 22, 2010, https://www.jaredgulian.com/2010/10/22/getting-intimate-with-a-cast-sheep/

[6] Keller, W. Phillip. *A Shepherd Looks at Psalm 23*. Zondervan, 2007, page 98.

[7] Keller, W. Phillip. *A Shepherd Looks at Psalm 23*. Zondervan, 2007, page 116.

[8] Keller, W. Phillip. *A Shepherd Looks at Psalm 23*. Zondervan, 2007, page 120.

[9] Keller, W. Phillip. *A Shepherd Looks at Psalm 23*. Zondervan, 2007, pages 139-143.